# THE EMPOWERED WOMAN

## PRAISE FOR *THE EMPOWERED WOMAN: 5 PRACTICES FOR INCREDIBLE SUCCESS*

*The Empowered Woman* is such a blessing. Dr. Chavonne beautifully reminds businesswomen that success isn't just about strategy—it's about alignment. She encourages us to take a practical and spiritual journey to examine how we're showing up in business and in life. This book is a must-read for any woman ready to walk in her purpose with clarity and confidence.
—**Elder Troia Butcher**, Founder & President of JustTroia, LLC

If you are stuck or think it is too late for you to walk in your destiny, this book is for you. *The Empowered Woman* is a powerful and inspiring read that speaks directly to the hearts and minds of women seeking to step into their full potential.

Dr. Stewart skillfully blends personal stories, practical tools, and motivational insights from her life with transparency to guide women on a journey of self-discovery, confidence-building, and purpose-driven living.

This book challenges you to know your worth, step into your greatness, and move from fear to faith and boldly walk into your calling. It is the book you MUST read!
—**Dr. Nancy J. Lewis**. President, Progressive Techniques, Inc.

Dr. Chavonne Stewart's book is an inspiring and faith-driven guide to achieving success in life and leadership. The book provides a well-structured approach to empowerment, rooted in biblical principles and practical strategies.

Through engaging storytelling and reflective exercises, Stewart encourages women to embrace their God-given strength, overcome obstacles, and develop a vision for their lives. Her emphasis on purpose, vision, and self-worth is particularly impactful, guiding readers toward self-discovery and confidence. The journal format makes this book interactive, allowing readers to personalize their journey and track their progress.

Stewart's integration of scripture reinforces the idea that faith and success go hand in hand, making this book ideal for those seeking spiritual and professional growth.

The writing is motivational and instructive, balancing encouragement with actionable advice. Readers will find themselves challenged to step outside their comfort zones and boldly pursue their aspirations.

Whether you are a businesswoman, entrepreneur, or simply someone looking to grow in leadership, this book offers a meaningful roadmap for transformation. *The Empowered Woman* is a powerful resource for women looking to embrace their full God-given potential and make a lasting impact.

**—Dr. Mashika Tempero-Culliver**, First Lady of Historic Tabernacle Baptist Church Selma, AL & Educator

This interactive book written by Dr. Chavonne Stewart is what women need to help write the vision and make it plain. Whether in ministry or in the marketplace, this book is essential to propel you to your next level. Get ready as you go on this journey to pinpoint God's purpose for your life.

**—Bernadette Dennis**, Founder & President of Ignite Revivals Ministry & Bernadette Dennis Entreprises, LLC

Dr. Stewart is not just another writer and researcher. She is a deeply perceptive and intuitive thought leader who has a passion to see transactions segue into transformations!

Her book will remind you of things you already know and challenge you with new ideas and concepts. Her galvanized knowledge and cathartic acumen will inspire and encourage you no matter what stage in life you are! This is the book, opportunity and season for change!

**—Dr. Brian Keith Hodges**, Sr, Bishop of Gathering of Champions Church, Marietta, GA, Dean, Center for Continuing Education, Professional Development, and Lifelong Learning, Beulah Heights University, Atlanta, GA

The title *The Empowered Woman* perfectly encapsulates this book's profound impact on many women in the years to come! Dr. Stewart's practices will guide you and inspire you to trust wholeheartedly in God's word. She boldly highlights the necessity of digging deep to gain insights that reveal your true purpose and goals. After engaging with this book, you will confidently seek clarity and fully understand your vision without fear. I'm excited for you and fully support the empowerment of women everywhere.

**—Dr. Telecia Stanton**, founder and president of Dreamz2Success, Inc.

*The Empowered Woman* is a critical arsenal for anyone searching for their purpose and the motivation to pursue it. This transformative read has plentiful scriptures and practical exercises to set even the most perplexed on a sure path to their destiny.

**—Deena C. M. Wingard**, J.D., M.Div., Pastor of Shekinah Greater Love Tabernacle, Inc & Founder of Your Reasonable Service Ministries, LLC

# THE EMPOWERED WOMAN

## 5 PRACTICES FOR INCREDIBLE SUCCESS

Dr. Chavonne D. Stewart

# COPYRIGHT NOTICE

*The Empowered Woman: 5 Practices for Incredible Success*
First edition. Copyright © 2025 Chavonne D. Stewart. The information contained in this book is the intellectual property of Chavonne D. Stewart and is governed by United States and International copyright laws. All rights reserved. No part of this publication, either text or image, may be used for any purpose other than personal use. Therefore, reproduction, modification, storage in a retrieval system, or retransmission, in any form or by any means, electronic, mechanical, or otherwise, for reasons other than personal use, except for brief quotations for reviews or articles and promotions, is strictly prohibited without prior written permission by the publisher.

Scripture marked NASB is taken from the New American Standard Bible © Copyright 1960, 1962, 1963, 1968, 1971, 1972, 1973, 1975, 1977 by the Lockman Foundation. Used with permission.

Scripture marked ESV is taken from The Holy Bible, English Standard Version. ESV® Text Edition: 2016. Copyright © 2001 by Crossway Bibles, a publishing ministry of Good News Publishers.

Scripture marked NKJV is taken from the New King James Version®. Copyright © 1982 by Thomas Nelson. Used by permission. All rights reserved.

Scripture marked NLT is taken from the Holy Bible, New Living Translation, copyright © 1996, 2004, 2007, 2013, 2015 by Tyndale House Foundation. Used by permission of Tyndale House Publishers Inc., Carol Stream, Illinois 60188. All rights reserved.

Cover and Interior Design: Derinda Babcock

Editor(s): Peggy Bodde

PUBLISHED BY: Dogwood Farms Publications, LLC, Email: dogwoodfrmspub@gmail.com, www.chavonnestewart.com or www.globalleadershiptechniques.com, 2025

---

Library Cataloging Data

Names: Stewart, Chavonne D. (Chavonne D. Stewart)

*The Empowered Woman: 5 Practices for Incredible Success* / Chavonne D. Stewart

68 p. 23cm × 15cm (9in × 6 in.)

ISBN-13:978-1-7338206-6-0 (paperback) | 978-1-7338206-3-9 (trade paperback) | 978-1-7338206-5-3 (trade hardcover) | 978-1-7338206-4-6 (e-book)

Key Words: personal growth books for women; empowering books for women; leadership books for women; personal growth for women; women empowering books; books for introverts

Library of Congress Control Number: 2025909231 Nonfiction

## DEDICATED TO ...

Every woman who has ever been told she is not enough, that she cannot achieve, or that she will never amount to anything; to those who have felt the weight of doubt or questioned their place in the world—this book is for you. May you find the courage to rise, the wisdom to lead, and the strength to step into every space God has called you to. Whether you are building a business, preaching from a pulpit, leading in the boardroom, or mentoring the next generation, know that you are equipped, empowered, and set apart for such a time as this.

To the trailblazers, the pioneers, and the silent warriors whose sacrifices paved the way for others—your resilience and faith continue to inspire. To my sisters in ministry and the marketplace, may this book serve as a reminder that success is not defined by titles or positions but by the impact we make and the lives we touch. Walk boldly, serve faithfully, and never shrink back from the greatness within you.

I would be remiss if I did not dedicate this section to my first mentor, sister, and friend, Elder Barbara Jones; affectionately known as "Barbs." Though gone too soon—but always in God's perfect timing—I would not be where I am without your training, guidance, and unwavering push for excellence. Serving alongside you in the Christian education department was truly an honor. You exemplified grace, power, and wisdom. I love and miss you dearly.

## CONTENTS

Praise for *The Empowered Woman: 5 Practices for Incredible Success*............................................... ii

Copyright Notice ............................... vi

Dedicated To ... ................................ vii

Introduction.................................... xi

Chapter 1: Know Your Purpose ..................... 1

JOURNAL ACTIVITY............................ 4

Chapter 2: Know Your Worth..................... 11

JOURNAL ACTIVITY........................... 14

Chapter 3: Invest in Yourself..................... 21

JOURNAL ACTIVITY........................... 24

Chapter 4: Build Your Network .................. 29

JOURNAL ACTIVITY........................... 31

Chapter 5: Build Your Legacy ................... 37

JOURNAL ACTIVITY........................... 39

Conclusion..................................... 47

Acknowledgement . . . . . . . . . . . . . . . . . . . . . . . . . . . . . 49

About the Author . . . . . . . . . . . . . . . . . . . . . . . . . . . . . . 51

Other Books by Dr. Chavonne D. Stewart . . . . . . . . . . . 53

Endnotes . . . . . . . . . . . . . . . . . . . . . . . . . . . . . . . . . . . . 55

# INTRODUCTION

"Attract what you expect, reflect what you desire, become what you respect, and mirror what you admire." **—Deb Sofield**[1]

Being empowered means stepping into the strength and authority that God has given you, fully trusting in His guidance and purpose for your life. It's about recognizing the power within you to overcome challenges, pursue your calling, and impact the world around you. Scripture reminds us of this empowerment in Philippians 4:13, "I can do all things through Christ who gives me strength." Empowerment means leaning on God's strength, embracing His plan for you, and confidently walking forward in faith, knowing that He has equipped you for every task ahead. How can you embrace this empowerment and live boldly in the purpose He has set for you?

If you're looking for answers, you're in the right place. Following the principles in this book will help you see yourself differently and understand what it means to embrace empowerment. I based this book on the empowering principles I shared in a presentation I created called "Five Ways to Become an Empowered Businesswoman." Afterwards, I felt compelled to expand the message, so, I decided to write a book on the topic. My goal is to guide women in business, leadership, and entrepreneurship. I want to support women in achieving success, growing in confidence, and making an impact in their personal and professional lives.

*The Empowered Woman: 5 Practices for Incredible Success* is designed to help women recognize their God-given strength and purpose in every season of life. By understanding the power that lies within, women can embrace their unique abilities, overcome challenges, and lead with confidence and resilience. The journey to empowerment begins with the understanding that you are fearfully and wonderfully made (see Psalm 139:14), and you are equipped with everything you need to thrive. You will be encouraged to rise above any obstacles as you seek and trust God's plan for you and confidently pursue the dreams He has placed in your heart. As you move forward, remember that empowerment is not just about personal success, but about lifting each other up and making a lasting impact in the world.

I designed this book as both a guide and a journal to help you reflect, reevaluate, and reset your mindset. It's not just meant to be read; it's meant to be written in. As you work through the pages, you'll find space to capture your thoughts, insights, and personal breakthroughs. The purpose of this format is to create a lasting reference tool, one that you can turn to whenever you feel discouraged or need to realign with your purpose. By combining practical guidance with personal reflection, this book will empower you to revisit your journey, celebrate your progress, and stay focused on your path forward. Are you ready to be empowered? Let's Go!

## CHAPTER 1: KNOW YOUR PURPOSE

"Be brave enough to live the life of your dreams according to your vision and purpose instead of the expectations and opinions of others." —**Roy T. Bennett**[2]

If you ever doubted that you have a purpose, let me begin by giving you two key scriptures that say you do:

"Before I formed you in the womb I knew you, and before you were born, I consecrated you," Jeremiah 1:5a.

'For I know the plans I have for you,' declares the Lord, 'plans to prosper you and not to harm you, plans to give you a future and a hope. Jeremiah 29:11.

The beauty of true purpose is that it comes from God and not man. Because it comes from God, nothing in this world can alter it. You have the responsibility to seek God wholeheartedly to gain clarity on your purpose in His Kingdom and how it manifests in the natural. In this chapter, you have several tasks to complete. You will define your purpose, identify long-term aspirations, and develop a vision and clear goals.

You will also explore the profound concept of purpose—what it truly means to live with intention and clarity in both your personal and professional lives. Purpose gives meaning to efforts and actions. It aligns your efforts with your vision, ensuring that activities contribute to a broader goal. Understanding your purpose is the foundation for identifying your long-term aspirations and creating a vision that guides you through life's journey.

Recognizing and knowing your purpose is important and will help you clearly define your vision. *But Dr. Chavonne!* I hear you. You're still processing the concept of having a purpose and now you have to develop a vision. Maybe you're asking, "Why do I need a vision?"

Let me begin by sharing what is in the Word of God. "Where there is no vision, the people perish," Proverbs 29:18. You can have a purpose, but if there is no vision for how the purpose will be fulfilled, you will perish. A vision is a clear picture of the future you want to achieve. It gives direction, fuels your passion, and ensures that every step you take aligns with your core values and calling. I'll take it one step further, Habakkuk 2:2 says, "Write the vision and make it plain on tablets; That he may run who reads it, (NKJV)." Not only do you need to understand your purpose and have a vision, but you need to put it in writing. Why? Because it gives you a constant reminder of your next steps and what you are working to accomplish.

Finally, the Bible reminds us in 1 Peter 2:9 that "you are a chosen generation, a royal priesthood, a holy nation, His own special people, that you may proclaim the praises of Him who called you out of darkness into His marvelous light," (NKJV). Here Peter reinforces the significance of understanding who we are and the greater purpose we serve. Living a purposeful life is not just about achieving goals; it's about honoring your calling and using your gifts to make a meaningful impact in the world.

If you still have questions, I understand. But let me finish; I'm not asking you to do anything that I haven't already done. In the last quarter of 2024, I reviewed and redefined my vision. My vision statement is this: "I will become a globally recognized leader in transformational coaching and leadership education, empowering women to lead with confidence, authenticity, and excellence in every sphere of influence, while building a financially thriving and impactful business." For me it was about clarity. I know my purpose, I'm like the Prophet Isaiah, a vocal piece for God's Kingdom. I move, live, and stand on this verse from Isaiah:

> Also, I heard the voice of the Lord, saying:
> "Whom shall I send, And who will go for Us?"
> Then I said, "Here am I! Send me!
> Isaiah 6:8 (NKJV)

I'm to be on the go always, proclaiming the Lord's word, fulfilling my purpose as a global leader who impacts the ministry and marketplace. I believe my vision is the blueprint that will help me fulfill my goal of becoming a full-time entrepreneur. Goals are specific, measurable objectives that you want to accomplish within a certain timeframe. They break down your vision into actionable steps. One intermediary goal I plan to achieve this year is to build my brand. An older goal I achieved a while ago was to complete my undergraduate degree. At the age of 24, I decided to go back to school. For four years, I worked and went to school full-time. This was challenging but fulfilling because I knew that completing my degree was the steppingstone to career elevation. Completing this goal took me a step further in achieving my vision and purpose.

So, what is your purpose? What's your vision? Your journey begins now! In the next section, you will discover God's purpose and take the next step to fulfill your true potential. It's time to take your career to new heights. No more fear or doubt, step out of the box!

## JOURNAL ACTIVITY

1. **Define your purpose and long-term aspirations, both professionally and personally. Start by seeking the Lord in prayer, then answer the questions.**
    - What is your true purpose, and how does it align with both your personal and professional aspirations?

_____
_____
_____
_____
_____
_____
_____
_____
_____
_____
_____
_____
_____
_____
_____
_____
_____
_____
_____
_____

- How do your values and passions shape your long-term vision, and how can you align your daily actions with that purpose?

- How do you define success in both your personal and professional life and what role does purpose play in achieving that success?

## 2. Develop a vision and clear goals.
- What is your vision for the next 5, 10, or 20 years, and how do you see yourself evolving along the way?

- What specific, measurable goals will help you bring your vision to life, and how will you hold yourself accountable to those goals?

- How can you break down your long-term aspirations into achievable milestones that will keep you motivated and focused on your journey?

_____
_____
_____
_____
_____
_____
_____
_____
_____
_____
_____
_____
_____
_____
_____
_____
_____
_____
_____
_____
_____
_____
_____

- In what ways can you adapt your goals and vision as circumstances change, while still staying true to your purpose?

_____

**TIP:** Break your goals down into actionable steps and establish milestones to track progress and regularly revisit your goals and vision. This will ensure alignment with your evolving ambitions.

## CHAPTER 2: KNOW YOUR WORTH

"Greatness lies within you. Your value has no limits. Impact begins inside of you. If you want others to value you, first, you have to value yourself."—**Bob Proctor**[3]

Do you feel that you now have a greater understanding of the significance of purpose? Are you in a place of comfort knowing that you have a purpose? I hope so. I remember the day of my revelation. God told me to stop doubting His voice. Sometimes we know He's guiding us, but we second-guess ourselves. Are you ready for the next phase in your journey? Let's go!

In this chapter, you will explore the importance of understanding your worth. Knowing your worth starts with being aware of yourself. You start by recognizing both your strengths and areas for growth. By reflecting on your journey, you'll learn to celebrate your successes—no matter how small—and embrace setbacks as opportunities for growth, rather than sources of self-doubt. Here's an example:

Twenty-plus years ago, I decided I wanted to become a hairstylist. I left college and enrolled in a cosmetology program at a technical school where I excelled. Fulfilling a dream I had since high school, I graduated with honors and passed my state board examination on the first go-round. By the first of the new year, I was working at a spa salon owned by an African American couple. I made it, but not quite.

There were some internal challenges that I had never addressed which trickled into work. These challenges were the fear of not being good enough and the fear of promoting myself via marketing. Back then, I struggled with tooting my own horn and knowing my worth. After nine years of being in the industry, I had an unexpected ending that caused me to struggle with failure. One day, I arrived at the salon for work, and after spending most of the day there, the owner informed me that I was being let go. As a commissioned stylist, the booth wasn't consistently generating enough income. I was blindsided and overwhelmed with embarrassment and humiliation. I quickly packed my things, ready to leave. I never saw it coming and had no time to prepare for it. In time, I came to understand the decision, but in that moment, the dream I had built seemed to crumble right before me. The fear of not being good enough, coupled with the uncertainty of how to promote myself and grow my business, was overwhelming. I realized that self-promotion is essential, and sometimes, you have to "toot your own horn," especially in front of potential clients.

I had a vision of owning an upscale salon, but I failed to factor myself into the equation. Did I have the mindset needed to achieve? Did I have the support or network? (We will talk about having a network in a later chapter.) I still walk in victory. Despite the setback, I never lost my entrepreneurial mindset. I learned how to adapt and recognized there was so much more within me. Over the past 10 years, I've discovered new talents and worked diligently to develop those skills. While my love for the beauty industry remains, I've grown into a successful self-published author and now run a consulting and coaching business. I am more confident in myself today than I ever was in my twenties. Praise the Lord!

Failure tried to defeat me, but God always provides a way—He places people in your path who encourage and push you toward greatness. I've learned that failure is not the end, but a training ground. Now, I view failure through a new lens. Instead of letting it defeat me, I ask myself: What can I learn from this? How can I grow? What lessons can I apply to avoid making the same mistakes again?

My dream crumbled, and as a result, I changed my career path. I don't want the same thing to happen to you! I don't want you to quit. Instead, I want to motivate you to learn and know your worth. Here are some ways to start the process.

Achieving a healthy work-life balance is key, and this requires setting clear boundaries and mastering time management. Equally important is nurturing your physical, mental, and emotional well-being through activities that support your overall health. Do you have a hobby? What is it and how often do you perform it? Here are some things I do. I walk at least four to five days a week. A colleague asked me if I had a hobby. He didn't know it at the time, but I had already thought about finding something I would enjoy regularly. He motivated me to do so. So, I started learning how to play pickleball and I enjoy it.

Another hobby happened when someone recommended the Duolingo App. I took Spanish for four years in high school and one semester in college. I always wanted to be fluent, so I started practicing with Duolingo. I've been working on my Spanish for over a year. Spain, here I come!

By cultivating confidence, resilience, and adaptability, you will develop a growth mindset that empowers you to thrive. Just think about how well you could lead a team in the workplace with the right amount of confidence. One way to grow your confidence is to ask yourself, "What are my likes and dislikes?" Have you ever wondered why you do certain things, for example, you get up every Sunday morning to go to church. I'm not saying don't go but ask yourself why. Are you going for you or someone else?

Another trap that women tend to fall into is dating men who do not care about them. This happens when we lack self-worth. Knowing your worth means you have an internal sense of self-value. You recognize that you are worthy and deserving of sincere love, respect, and belonging.

Lastly, I will leave you with this thought. God's word is the truth. Scripture reminds us of our inherent worth in God's eyes: "So God created mankind in his own image, in the image of God he created them; male and female he created them" (Genesis 1:27). Understanding that you are created in His image anchors you in the knowledge that you are valuable, loved, and capable of growing in every aspect of your life.

## JOURNAL ACTIVITY

1. **Self-Awareness and Strengths**
    - What unique strengths and skills do you bring to your personal and professional life? How have they contributed to your success?

_____
_____
_____
_____
_____
_____
_____
_____
_____
_____

- Think of a time when you felt most confident and in control. What strengths did you lean on during that moment?

- Identify areas where growth is needed.

_____
_____
_____
_____
_____
_____
_____
_____
_____

2. **Celebrating Success and Learning from Setbacks**
    - Reflect on your proudest achievements in the last 3-5 years. What made these moments meaningful to you?

_____
_____
_____
_____
_____
_____
_____
_____
_____
_____
_____
_____

- How have you celebrated your recent successes, and how can you make a habit of acknowledging your wins, big or small?

___

- Share an example of a setback or challenge you've faced. What valuable lessons did you take away, and how did you grow from the experience?

___

3. **Work-Life Balance and Boundaries**
   - What strategies have you found effective in managing your time between work, family, and personal commitments?

_____
_____
_____
_____
_____
_____
_____
_____
_____
_____
_____

4. **Nurturing Well-being**
   - If you were to dedicate thirty minutes each day to self-care, what would that look like for you?

_____
_____
_____
_____
_____
_____
_____
_____

5. **Confidence, Resilience, and Growth**
   - Can you share a time when you demonstrated resilience in the face of adversity? What helped you persevere?

   _____
   _____
   _____
   _____
   _____
   _____
   _____
   _____
   _____
   _____
   _____

   - What steps are you currently taking to cultivate a growth mindset and embrace challenges as opportunities?

   _____
   _____
   _____
   _____
   _____
   _____
   _____

6. **Exploring Hobbies and Interests**
   - Imagine you could try three new activities or hobbies in the next six months. What would they be, and what excites you about them?

## CHAPTER 3: INVEST IN YOURSELF

Investing in yourself is the best thing you can do.
—**Warren Buffet**[4]

Are you ready to take the next step forward? It is time to invest in yourself. Ladies, we are going to go deeper. Typically, women wear multiple hats, focusing on helping others. I am not undermining the value of serving. God desires that all would serve. But when you forget about yourself in the process, that becomes a problem. When was the last time you made an investment in yourself? What does this even mean? It means allocating the time, effort, and resources towards your professional and personal growth and development. When we invest in ourselves first, we can positively impact the lives of others.

Keep in mind that investing is not just about finances—it's about committing to your personal and professional growth. In this chapter, we will explore how to invest in yourself. One way you can start is through continuous learning and development. Staying updated with industry trends and advancements through courses, certifications, and seminars is key to remaining competitive and adaptable. Building expertise in essential areas such as leadership, negotiation, and financial management will empower you to take on greater challenges and opportunities. Embracing a mindset of lifelong learning allows you to evolve, grow, and rise to new heights. You can then turn every challenge into a chance to strengthen your skills and broaden your knowledge. I will use myself as an example.

While working as a part-time hairstylist, I also managed the family business. It was during this time that I decided to finish my degree. As mentioned earlier, it does not matter when you start as long as you finish. This time around, I studied what I enjoyed which was history. Putting myself first, I made the investment (and sacrifice) for my education, and as a result, I graduated with an undergraduate degree in 2007. As a side note, I would have graduated with overall honors had I not messed up the first time I was in college. Obtaining my undergraduate degree was a significant personal achievement for me. It represented both a sense of accomplishment and a steppingstone for professional growth and new opportunities. The first time I attended college, I didn't drop out because I couldn't handle the work; rather, I wanted to pursue a different goal at that time. I wasn't fully invested in the idea of being in college—I went because my parents told me I had to. My heart wasn't in it.

However, the second time around, things were different. I returned to college because I, Chavonne, genuinely wanted to achieve this goal for myself. There's a huge difference when you do something because it's expected of you versus when you do it because you desire it for your own growth and success. The shift in mindset made all the difference. When I approached my studies with intention and passion, I excelled in every aspect. I finally saw the true value of investing in my education, not just for a degree, but for personal fulfillment and long-term success.

Here's another perspective on investing in yourself. Maybe college isn't the right path for everyone, but a good book can change your life. As a life, business, and career coach, I'm passionate about building and empowering strong leaders. Before I can help others grow, I prioritize materials that help me grow personally. Right now, I'm reading Trust by Dr. Henry Cloud, which offers a comprehensive look at trust—teaching us not only when to trust, but also when to be cautious. Of course, we should always trust God, but Dr. Cloud's insights have been invaluable.

I've also read many other books that have shaped my leadership journey, like those by John Maxwell, *The Art of Possibility* by Rosamund and Benjamin Zander, and *The 7 Habits of Highly Effective People*, just to name a few. These books, along with countless others on ministry, have enriched my understanding of leadership.

The point is, the more knowledge you acquire, the more power you gain when you apply that knowledge. You can't effectively lead a team without knowledge and understanding—it's like the blind leading the blind. I have a friend I call a "super reader" because he can finish a book in just 2-3 days. I'm not a super reader; I take my time and digest the material slowly. But the key is that I'm doing it, and so can you.

Investing in yourself is the greatest investment you will ever make. The knowledge and growth you gain will not only transform you but will empower you to lead and make a lasting impact on others. Personal achievement is key to our sustainability and success because it empowers us to create goals that align with our deepest desires. When we pursue what truly matters to us, we are more committed, focused, and resilient in overcoming obstacles. It becomes less about meeting external expectations and more about fostering growth that sustains us through challenges and drives us toward new opportunities.

But we live and learn. If you want change in your life professionally or personally, you must be willing to make the investment for that change to happen. What investments are you willing to make?

## JOURNAL ACTIVITY

1. **Stay updated with industry trends and advancements through courses, certifications, and seminars.**
   - How do you currently stay informed about the latest trends and advancements in your industry, and what steps can you take to deepen your knowledge?

_____
_____
_____
_____
_____
_____
_____
_____
_____
_____
_____
_____
_____
_____
_____
_____
_____
_____

- How can you leverage industry events to not only stay updated but also connect with thought leaders and innovators?

___

- What have you done recently to invest in your career, and what additional actions can you take to accelerate your professional growth?

___

2. **Build your expertise in areas such as leadership, negotiation, and financial management.**
   - What concrete actions are you taking to strengthen your expertise in these key areas?

   _____
   _____
   _____
   _____
   _____
   _____
   _____
   _____
   _____
   _____
   _____

   - In which of these areas do you feel you could improve the most, and what resources will help you accelerate your growth?

   _____
   _____
   _____
   _____
   _____
   _____
   _____
   _____
   _____
   _____

3. **Cultivate a mindset of lifelong learning, embracing new challenges and knowledge.**
    - How can you cultivate a mindset that welcomes continuous learning and seeks out new challenges, professionally and personally?

    _____
    _____
    _____
    _____
    _____
    _____
    _____
    _____
    _____
    _____

    - In what ways can you embrace failure as part of your learning process, and how will this mindset help you grow in your career?

    _____
    _____
    _____
    _____
    _____
    _____
    _____
    _____
    _____
    _____

# THE EMPOWERED WOMAN

## CHAPTER 4: BUILD YOUR NETWORK

*Your network is your net worth.* —**Porter Gale**[5]

On New Year's Eve, I attended a church service, and the bishop ministered a phenomenal word about the "Power of Connection!" The foundation scripture for his message was John 15, abiding in the vine. Who are you connected to? God, the Father is the vinedresser, Jesus is the vine, and we are the branches. What a powerful connection!

Staying connected to the vine means we have life and creativity; we can achieve; and we are fruit bearers. It is important to stay connected and networked with God, and we must do the same in the earth realm. Being connected to the right people will help propel us into our destinies. In this chapter, we will explore the power of building a strong, supportive network that can move you forward in your personal and professional life.

Surrounding yourself with mentors, coaches, peers, therapists, and professionals who inspire and challenge you is imperative for growth. You can leverage networking events, professional organizations, and social platforms to create meaningful connections. By establishing relationships that offer mutual support, guidance, and collaboration opportunities, you can unlock new possibilities, create a foundation for long-term personal success, and use what you learn to improve the workplace environment.

Your network isn't just about who you know—it's about the value you bring and the growth you inspire together. Let me be real with you: this section may be a challenge for you. If you are like me, (an introvert), you may struggle to connect with people. But I am here to tell you, you can do it. I encourage you to pray about it, and the Lord will put you in a position to meet people you never expected to meet.

In my opinion, introverts need to be more intentional about building connections. I'm part of the Transforming Women Entrepreneurs (TWE) monthly prayer call, and through that, I've had the privilege of connecting with some powerful women of God who are making waves in the marketplace. These women are influencing various spheres of society—such as religion, arts and entertainment, media, business, family, and more.

Through these connections, I've been blessed to collaborate with one of my TWE sisters on this book: P. Bodde, a highly accomplished author, editor, entrepreneur, and wife, who has generously offered her expertise in editing my story. What's even more remarkable is that we've never met in person. Thank God for Zoom! This experience has shown me the power of being intentional about connecting, no matter where we are.

Five years ago, during the COVID pandemic, I started working with a consulting firm. The CEO of the firm said, "Chavonne, I want to connect you with one of my consultants." He recognized that we had something big in common—our faith. After connecting, we became prayer partners, as she hosts the TWE monthly prayer call for entrepreneurs—a connection I've mentioned before. I have been invited to be a guest on her television show and more.

This unexpected connection pushed me further out of my comfort zone. I was hesitant at first but chose to remain open to it. I'll be the first to admit, I struggle with trusting people. Despite this, I work hard not to let that struggle hinder me. I remind myself constantly that I need to trust the Lord in all that I do—seeking Him first for guidance. I've learned to discern the spirit of the people around me and to ask God, "Is this someone I need to align myself with?"

I've also come to realize that Chavonne, who can be a bit of a loner at times, cannot work or achieve greatness in isolation. It takes a network. Jesus himself fulfilled His mission on earth, but He knew there was more work to be done. So, He immediately began handpicking individuals to carry on the work once He left. Over the centuries, this has created a domino effect, with the Gospel continuing to spread. The same principle applies in business. Through our connections, we meet people and glean wisdom from others.

I also believe the number-one principle in marketing is "word of mouth." Our connections can determine who we meet and whose table we sit at. Someone speaks for you, just as Jesus speaks and intercedes for us in heaven. It's all about the power of relationships and the impact they have on our personal and professional journeys.

From this one connection, I am connected to many other women in business. I am part of two networks: Transforming Women Entrepreneur's and Women About Biz. Being an introvert should never stop you, and it does not mean you cannot be a successful entrepreneur. You simply process information differently, and you must be willing to step out of your comfort zone. I hope what I shared has empowered you to build your network. In this section, I want you to take the time to ask yourself these questions.

## JOURNAL ACTIVITY

1. **Surround yourself with mentors, peers, and professionals who inspire and challenge you.**

- Who are the individuals in your life who inspire and challenge you to be your best self, and how can you strengthen those relationships?

_____
_____
_____
_____
_____
_____
_____
_____
_____
_____
_____

- How can you actively seek out mentors and peers who will help you grow, both personally and professionally?

_____
_____
_____
_____
_____
_____
_____
_____
_____
_____
_____

- What qualities do you value most in mentors or colleagues, and how can you identify those who align with your growth aspirations?

_____
_____
_____
_____
_____
_____
_____
_____
_____
_____
_____
_____

2. **Attend networking events, join professional organizations, and leverage social platforms.**
   - How can you expand your network by attending events or joining organizations that align with your professional goals?

_____
_____
_____
_____
_____
_____
_____
_____

- What steps can you take to leverage social platforms more effectively to connect with like-minded professionals and broaden your reach?

- How do you prepare yourself to make meaningful connections at networking events and maximize their potential?

3. **Establish relationships that provide mutual support, guidance, and collaboration opportunities.**
   - What does a mutually supportive relationship look like, and how can you create one with the people you engage with professionally?

- How can you foster collaboration within your network to create win-win opportunities for everyone involved?

_____
_____
_____
_____
_____
_____
_____
_____
_____
_____

- What actions can you take to ensure that your professional relationships are built on trust, respect, and a shared vision for success?

_____
_____
_____
_____
_____
_____
_____
_____
_____
_____

## CHAPTER 5: BUILD YOUR LEGACY

> The greatest legacy one can pass on to one's children and grandchildren is not money ... but rather a legacy of character and faith."—**Billy Graham**[6]

Welcome to Chapter Five; you have come full circle. Now that you recognize your purpose, know your worth and the value of investing in yourself and building your network, it's time to think about the legacy you will leave. Let's start the building process. First, legacy is not always about money. Here are some examples from the Bible of women who left a legacy.

Mary, the mother of Jesus was the epitome of faith and obedience—traits we can carry forward in our own lives. Ruth was faithful and as a result, became part of Jesus' lineage. Sarah was committed to her family, and she loved and respected Abraham. Abigail was a woman of integrity and dignity, and Deborah was an influential judge. Jael was fearless and courageous. Stop and think about what has been shared. The legacy of each biblical woman extends way beyond financial gain; it speaks to their character.

Passing down specific character traits is the foundation for lasting legacies. In this chapter, we will focus on the importance of building a legacy that lasts beyond your lifetime. You'll learn how to make a meaningful impact that influences future generations, fosters a culture of inclusivity, and advocates for those who may not have a voice.

By paying it forward and creating platforms of influence, you can inspire others to follow in your footsteps. Since you began this book, you have taken steps to ensure your legacy is sustainable, steps like defining purpose and writing your vision. As a result of the planning, you have created a positive change that will continue to grow and thrive for years to come. This chapter is the icing on the cake. Leaving a legacy gives future generations a foundation to stand on.

In preparation for this chapter, I asked my mom about her parents' legacy. She shared a few things such as her parents believing in education, family and marriage, going to church, and being hard workers. Let me take it a step further. Although my grandparents are no longer here, there are four generations present. Out of the siblings (my mom's sisters), three out of five have college degrees and two have certificates of training.

In my generation there were nine grandchildren. We all have college degrees, two of us have doctorates, and one has a master's. In every generation except for the fourth one (the toddlers), there are lasting marriages, successful entrepreneurs and careers, homeownership, and leaders within the church. Needless to say, my grandparents would be proud. Their legacy of faith, resilience, and hard work continues to thrive in us, a testament of the seeds they planted and the foundation they built for generations to come. Take a moment to reflect on the legacies within your own family or what you want to leave for future generations. Invite the Lord in and respond once you hear from Him.

## JOURNAL ACTIVITY

1. **Make a difference that impacts generations to come.**
   - What kind of impact do you want to have on future generations, and how can you begin making that difference today?

   _____
   _____
   _____
   _____
   _____
   _____
   _____
   _____
   _____
   _____

   - How can you align your actions, values, and decisions to create a lasting legacy that resonates with those who follow you?

   _____
   _____
   _____
   _____
   _____
   _____
   _____
   _____

- What steps can you take to ensure that the work you do today continues to inspire and benefit others long into the future?

2. **Foster a culture of inclusivity and advocate for others.**
    - How can you actively contribute to creating a more inclusive environment in your community or workplace?

    _____
    _____
    _____
    _____
    _____
    _____
    _____
    _____
    _____
    _____
    _____
    _____

    - Who can you advocate for, and what steps can you take to elevate their voices and experiences?

    _____
    _____
    _____
    _____
    _____
    _____
    _____
    _____
    _____

- In what ways can you challenge the status quo to foster a culture where everyone feels valued and heard?

3. **Pay it forward by creating platforms of influence.**
    - How can you use your skills, resources, and connections to create opportunities for others?

- What platforms, both formal and informal, can you build or leverage to help others grow and succeed?

_____
_____
_____
_____
_____
_____
_____
_____
_____
_____
_____

- How can you shift your mindset from individual success to collective empowerment, ensuring others have the tools they need to thrive?

_____
_____
_____
_____
_____
_____
_____
_____
_____

4. **Ensure your legacy is sustainable through careful planning and resource allocation.**
   - How can you strategically plan and allocate resources to ensure that your legacy is not only impactful but sustainable over time?

   _____
   _____
   _____
   _____
   _____
   _____
   _____
   _____
   _____
   _____
   _____

   - What tools, systems, or frameworks can you put in place to ensure that your work continues to support future generations?

   _____
   _____
   _____
   _____
   _____
   _____
   _____
   _____

- How can you ensure that your legacy is built on a foundation of sustainability, ethics, and responsibility?

# 46 | THE EMPOWERED WOMAN

# CONCLUSION

"The only person you are destined to become is the person you decide to be."—**Ralph Waldo Emerson**[7]

Do you feel empowered? Are you ready to take charge of your career or business? Are you ready to make an impact on the Kingdom of God? If you said "yes" to one or more of these questions, you are on your way to being an Empowered Woman! Empowerment is a journey that requires purpose, self-awareness, continuous learning, meaningful relationships, and a commitment to leaving a lasting impact. This book provides the foundation for becoming an empowered woman, ready to embrace challenges and opportunities with confidence and resilience.

As you move forward, remember that true empowerment is not just about personal achievement; it's about lifting others as you rise. Whether it's mentoring a colleague, building a thriving team, or serving your community with excellence, your growth has the potential to create a ripple effect of positive change. By aligning your goals with your faith, you can confidently step into leadership roles, knowing that your journey is guided by divine purpose. Embrace the tools and strategies shared in this book and let them propel you toward a future filled with success, significance, and service. The world is waiting for your unique impact—go forth and be unstoppable!

## ACKNOWLEDGEMENT

Living an empowered life on purpose is a steppingstone to total fulfillment and success. While each of our journeys may be different, the most important thing to remember is not how we start the race but how we finish it knowing we have achieved all God put us on this earth to do. One way we finish strong is by having the right people in our lives to motivate and inspire us, and God has blessed me in providing that.

First, I would like to thank God for choosing me to be an example for women in ministry and the marketplace. Thank you to my family and close friends for all your love, support, and encouragement. My prayer is that this book will bless and change every person who reads it. I hope that you, the reader, will apply the knowledge learned, so you can live an empowered life. Applied knowledge is power!

To A. Plant and T. Ivey: It is because of you that I am in the higher education position I currently hold. A. Plant, you mentored me, advocated on my behalf, and stood as an ally throughout my journey. T. Ivey, you specifically guided me through my dissertation process, ensuring I stayed on track and reached my goals. Both of you were the voices at the tables I had not yet been a part of, paving the way for me. For all of this and more, thank you.

# ABOUT THE AUTHOR

Education Consultant, Coach, Author, Speaker

Dr. Chavonne D. Stewart is the CEO of Global Leadership Techniques, LLC, and president of Watchmen International, Inc., a prayer and evangelism ministry. In addition to her entrepreneurial endeavors, she is the director of assessment and a business and leadership faculty member at Beulah Heights University in Atlanta, Georgia. She holds a Ph.D. in Organizational Leadership from Beulah Heights University, an MSc in Management from Troy University, a BA in History from Kennesaw State University, and a life-coach certification through DreamReleaser Coaching, LLC.

In addition to her academic pursuits and entrepreneurial endeavors, Dr. Stewart is an accomplished self-published author of five books, including the children's series *The Adventures of Amilya Rose*, and a contributor to three anthology series. In her spare time, she enjoys traveling, attending sporting events (Go Braves!), shopping, reading, and spending time with family.

> "Work hard in silence and let success make noise."—Frank Ocean[8]

## OTHER BOOKS BY DR. CHAVONNE D. STEWART

*Getting Started: Quick Guide to Become a Self-Published Author* (2018)

*In Him Affirmations: Who I am In Christ?* Devotion & Journal (2016)

*The Adventures of Amilya: Father-Daughter Dance* (June 2016)

*The Adventures of Amilya Rose: Disappearance* (August 2015)

*The Adventures of Amilya Rose: The Lie* (2014)

## ENDNOTES

1 https://debsofield.com/attract-what-you-expect-reflect-what-you-desire-become-what-you-respect-and-mirror-what-you-admire/

2 https://www.goodreads.com/quotes/7954061-live-the-life-of-your-dreams-be-brave-enough-to

3 Proctor, B. (2023). Born Rich. G & D Media

4 https://www.nasdaq.com/articles/warren-buffett-says-the-most-critical-investment-lies-within-ourselves

5 Gale, P. (2013). Your Network Is Your Net Worth: Unlock the Hidden Power of Connections for Wealth, Success, and Happiness in the Digital Age. Artia Books

6 https://www.brainyquote.com/quotes/billy_graham_626354

7 https://www.goodreads.com/quotes/73656-the-only-person-you-are-destined-to-become-is-the

8 https://www.goodreads.com/quotes/990324-work-hard-in-silence-let-your-success-be-your-noise

www.ingramcontent.com/pod-product-compliance
Lightning Source LLC
Chambersburg PA
CBHW061741070526
44585CB00024B/2761